COUNTRY PROFILES

SCOTLAND

BY ALICIA Z. KLEPEIS

BLASTOFF!
DISCOVERY

BELLWETHER MEDIA • MINNEAPOLIS, MN

Blastoff! Discovery launches a new mission: reading to learn. Filled with facts and features, each book offers you an exciting new world to explore!

This edition first published in 2020 by Bellwether Media, Inc.

Library of Congress Cataloging-in-Publication Data

Names: Klepeis, Alicia, 1971- author.
Title: Scotland / by Alicia Z. Klepeis.
Description: Minneapolis, MN : Bellwether Media, Inc., [2020] |
    Series: Blastoff! Discovery: Country Profiles | Includes bibliographical
    references and index. | Audience: Grades 3-8. | Audience:
    Ages 7-13.
Identifiers: LCCN 2019001640 (print) | LCCN 2019002134 (ebook)
    | ISBN 9781618915948 (ebook) | ISBN 9781644870532
    (hardcover : alk. paper)
Subjects: LCSH: Scotland–Juvenile literature.
Classification: LCC DA762 (ebook) | LCC DA762 .K55 2020 (print)
    | DDC 941.1–dc23
LC record available at https://lccn.loc.gov/2019001640

Editor: Rebecca Sabelko   Designer: Brittany McIntosh

Printed in the United States of America, North Mankato, MN.

TABLE OF CONTENTS

CAIRNGORMS NATIONAL PARK

It is a cool summer morning in Cairngorms National Park. A family heads out from their campsite by bike. Soon they arrive at **Loch** Morlich. They park their bikes and walk along the water's edge. Since the water feels chilly, they explore the lake in kayaks.

OTHER TOP SITES

EDINBURGH CASTLE

FORTH BRIDGE

ISLE OF LEWIS

LOCH NESS

LOCH MORLICH
CAIRNGORMS NATIONAL PARK

After a picnic lunch, the family hikes through the pine and spruce forest. They spot red squirrels scampering through the trees. Later in the day, they go for a drive. They pass by what looks like a carpet of purple heather. Before dinner they explore Corgarff Castle. Welcome to Scotland!

LOCATION

HUNDREDS OF ISLANDS

Scotland has more than 790 islands! People live on about 90 of the islands. Some, including the Isles of Skye and Islay, attract many visitors.

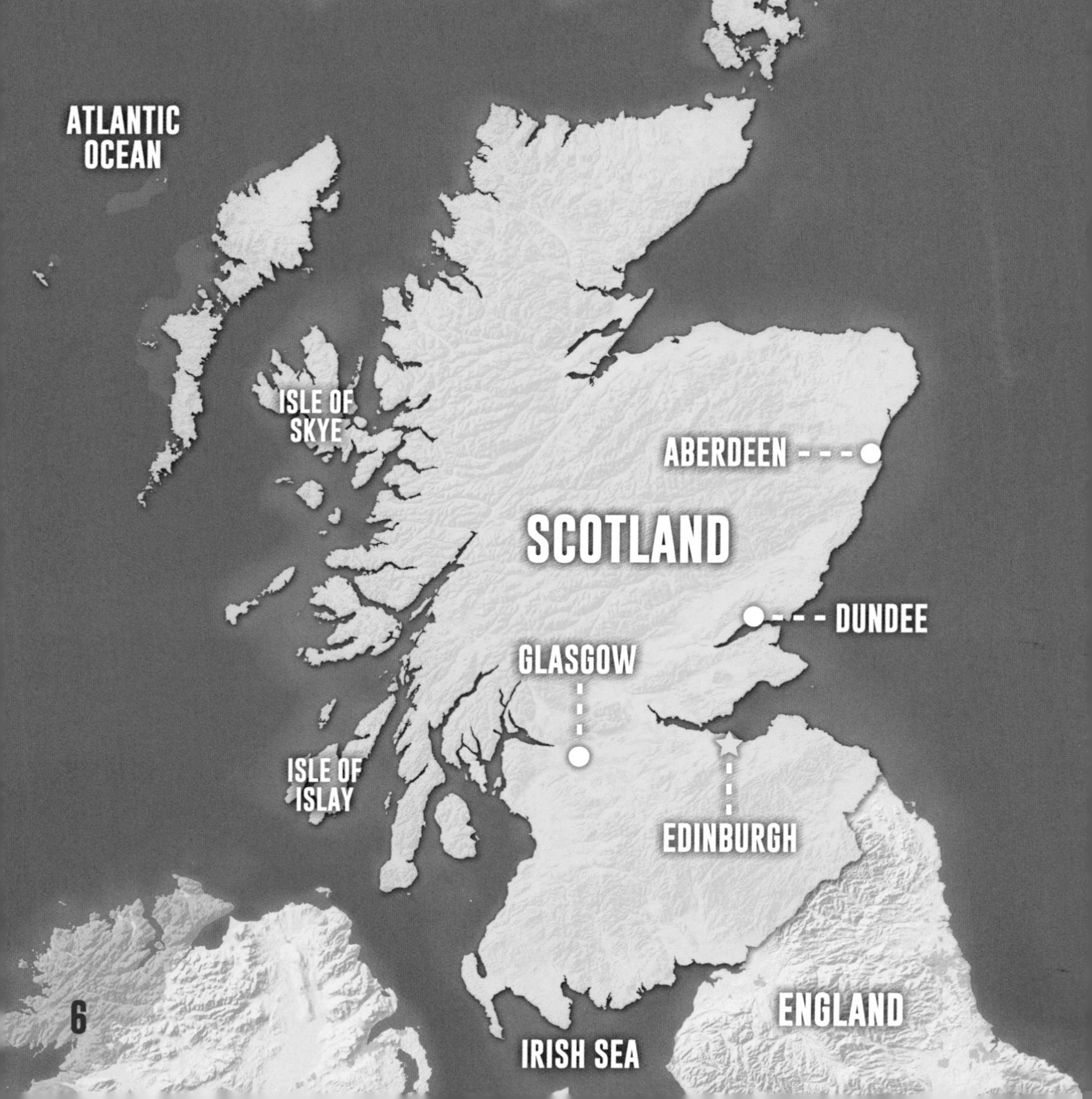

ATLANTIC OCEAN
ISLE OF SKYE
ABERDEEN
SCOTLAND
DUNDEE
GLASGOW
ISLE OF ISLAY
EDINBURGH
ENGLAND
IRISH SEA

N
W ＋ E
S

NORTH
SEA

Scotland is located in Europe on the island of Great Britain. It covers 30,414 square miles (78,772 square kilometers). Scotland is the northernmost country in the United Kingdom (U.K.). Wales, England, and Northern Ireland are also parts of the U.K.

Scotland's capital city, Edinburgh, lies on the country's east coast. The North Sea washes upon its shores. To the west and north, the Atlantic Ocean touches Scotland's coasts. Waves from the Irish Sea lap against the country's southern shores. England is Scotland's southern neighbor.

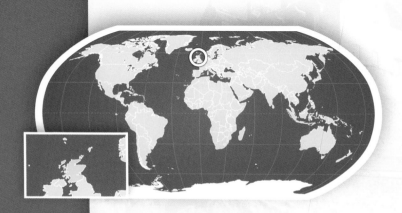

LANDSCAPE AND CLIMATE

Scotland's landscape can be divided into highlands, lowlands, and islands. Northern Scotland is home to seaside cliffs and steep valleys. The highlands are mostly filled by the Grampian Mountains. This range includes the U.K.'s highest point, Ben Nevis. South of the Grampians are the central lowlands. Rich farmland and thick forests stretch across this area. Southern Scotland has rolling hills and high **moorlands**.

= GRAMPIAN MOUNTAINS
= CENTRAL LOWLANDS

BEN NEVIS

N
W + E
S

BEN NEVIS

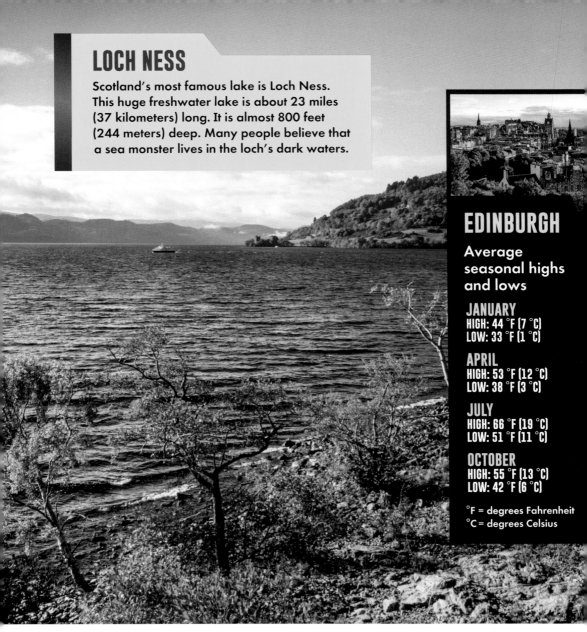

LOCH NESS

Scotland's most famous lake is Loch Ness. This huge freshwater lake is about 23 miles (37 kilometers) long. It is almost 800 feet (244 meters) deep. Many people believe that a sea monster lives in the loch's dark waters.

EDINBURGH

Average seasonal highs and lows

JANUARY
HIGH: 44 °F (7 °C)
LOW: 33 °F (1 °C)

APRIL
HIGH: 53 °F (12 °C)
LOW: 38 °F (3 °C)

JULY
HIGH: 66 °F (19 °C)
LOW: 51 °F (11 °C)

OCTOBER
HIGH: 55 °F (13 °C)
LOW: 42 °F (6 °C)

°F = degrees Fahrenheit
°C = degrees Celsius

Overall, Scotland has a cool and wet climate. It does not have temperature extremes during the year. The east coast tends to be drier than the west. The country's mountains often get snow in the winter.

WILDLIFE

Many kinds of wildlife live in Scotland. Seals and dolphins frolic in the waters off the country's west coast. Puffins and gannets fly overhead in search of fish and eels. Red deer and mountain hares scamper about in the Scottish mountains. They feed on grasses and tree bark.

Fuzzy pine martens wander through Scotland's forests. They eat everything from fruit and insects to small rodents. **Venomous** snakes called adders hunt birds that nest in Scotland's forests and moorlands. Curlews also dwell in the wet moors and grasslands.

GREY SEALS

RED DEER

PINE MARTEN

ATLANTIC PUFFIN

COMMON EUROPEAN ADDER

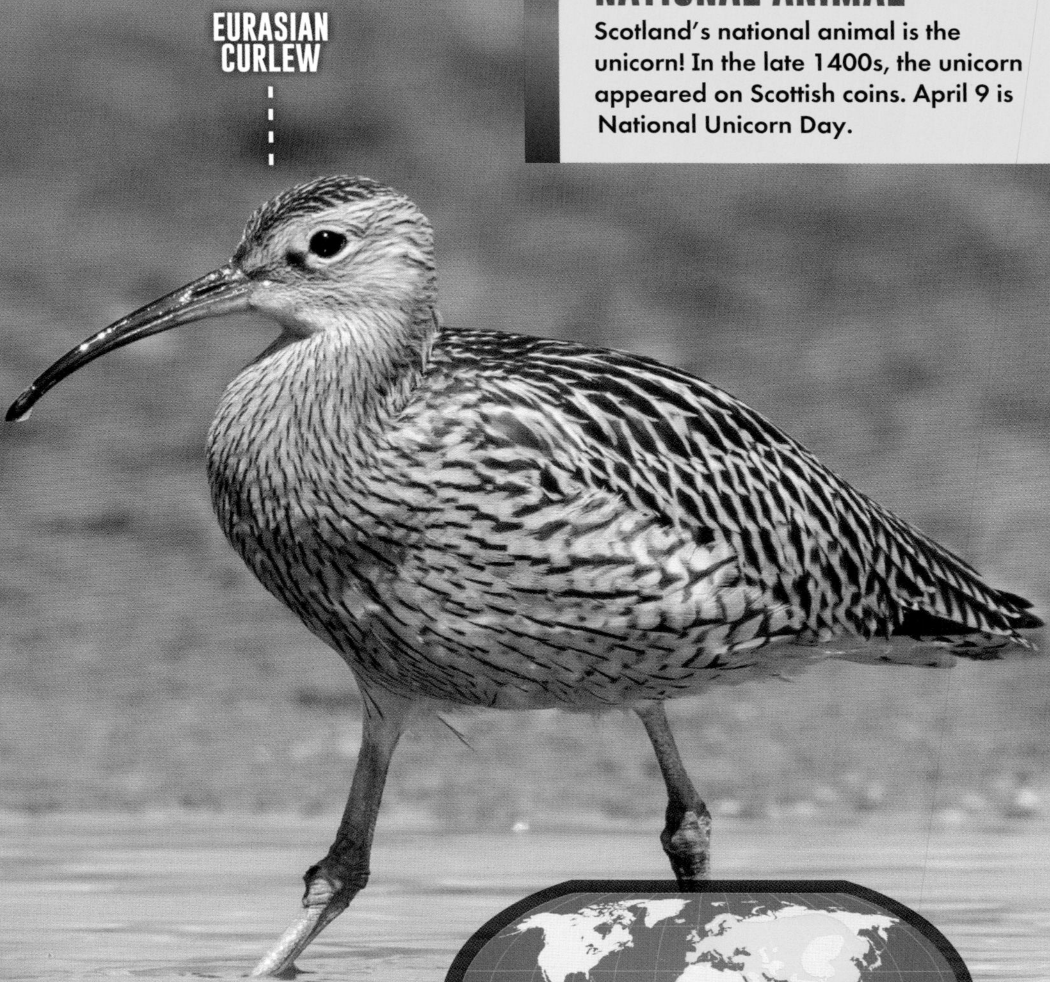

EURASIAN
CURLEW
: : : :
: : : :

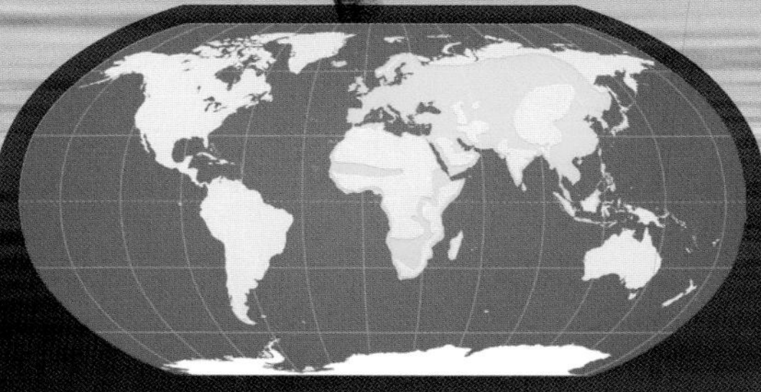

EURASIAN CURLEW

Life Span: **5 years**
Red List Status: **near threatened**

Eurasian curlew range = ▨

LEAST CONCERN	NEAR THREATENED	VULNERABLE	ENDANGERED	CRITICALLY ENDANGERED	EXTINCT IN THE WILD	EXTINCT
	▲					

More than 5 million people live in Scotland. They are referred to as Scots. Nearly two-thirds of the population come from a Scottish background. The next largest group of people identify as Scottish and British. A small number of Scotland's people are of Asian **descent**, many of whom are Pakistani. Scottish residents also include people of African, Caribbean, and other backgrounds.

Nearly half of Scots are Christian. The biggest group of Christians belong to the Church of Scotland. Islam is the most common religion after Christianity. However, many Scots follow no religion. The official languages of Scotland are English and Scottish Gaelic.

FAMOUS FACE

Name: Andy Murray
Birthday: May 15, 1987
Hometown: Glasgow, Scotland
Famous for: One of the world's top-ranked tennis players who won Olympic gold medals in men's singles in 2012 and 2016

SPEAK SCOTTISH GAELIC

ENGLISH	SCOTTISH GAELIC	HOW TO SAY IT
hello	halò	HAH-loh
goodbye	mar sin leibh	mahr shen LEH-eev
please	ma's e ur toil e	mah sheh oor TUL-leh
thank you	tapadh leibh	TAH-puh LEH-eev
yes	tha	HAH
no	chan eil	han yale

EDINBURGH

A majority of Scots live in cities, especially those between the ages of 16 and 34. This may be due to better educational and job opportunities in **urban** areas. City dwellers often live in apartments. People in Scottish cities often travel by bus or train.

A CITY OF MANY HONORS

Glasgow is Scotland's musical capital! It has also been named a European City of Culture and a City of Architecture and Design.

In the countryside, Scots may live far from their neighbors. **Rural** homes range from simple stone cottages to fancy estates or even castles. People may use cars or ferries to get around rural Scotland. But planes are the best way to reach the country's **remote** islands.

CEILIDH

People in villages across Scotland hold gatherings called *ceilidhs*. These parties feature Scottish folk music. **Traditional** Scottish dancers also perform. Sometimes hotels hold ceilidhs to entertain guests. Ceilidhs can also be part of wedding celebrations.

Scotland is famous for a fabric called tartan. It comes in many different colors and patterns of plaid. Tartan is usually woven from wool. It originally came from the Highlands of Scotland. Different **clans** wore different tartan patterns. A kilt is a skirt-like garment made from tartan. Today people often wear kilts at weddings and ceilidhs.

SCOTTISH BAGPIPES

Scotland's national instrument is the bagpipe. This wind instrument has four pipes. Three make a constant sound. One changes the pitch or chords. Music from the Scottish Highlands often features bagpipes.

BAGPIPE PLAYERS WEARING KILTS

Scotland provides free education for all children from ages 3 to 18. Kids often attend preschool before primary school. At the secondary level, some students prepare for university. They study the arts, health, math, languages, science, technology, and more. Others train for a variety of jobs.

Most people in Scotland have **service jobs**. Health care and **tourism** are two big employers. Other Scots **manufacture** products like medicines and lumber. Scottish foods and beverages are big moneymakers, too. Farmers grow barley, potatoes, fruits, and vegetables. They also raise livestock including cattle, sheep, and poultry.

FARMER

WIND ENERGY

Wind power is Scotland's biggest source of renewable energy. The world's first floating offshore wind farm is located in the North Sea. It started generating electricity in 2017.

SHINTY

Scotland's most popular sports are soccer and rugby. Scots enjoy watching these sports on television and at stadiums around the country. People also like golf and tennis. *Shinty* is a sport that started in Scotland. It is similar to field hockey.

RUGBY

The Highland Games are a huge **cultural** event held each summer. Sporting activities at this event include tug-o-war and caber toss. A caber is a huge tree trunk that weighs up to 180 pounds (82 kilograms). People compete to flip the caber as straight as possible! Traditional dancing and music are also part of the Highland Games. There is even a competition for the best-dressed pet.

CABER TOSS

DESIGN AN INDOOR GOLF COURSE

Scotland is home to some of the world's best golf courses!

What You Need:
- sticks (1 per player)
- cardboard
- scissors
- tape
- 6 small boxes
- a marker
- pillows and blankets
- a small ball

How to Play:
1. To make a golf club, cut out a small rectangle from the cardboard. Tape it to the bottom of a stick.
2. Number the small boxes one through six.
3. Cut six small squares from the cardboard and number them one through six. These are your tees.
4. Place the boxes around the room and pick a tee spot for each box. Use pillows and blankets to create your course.
5. Starting at tee number one, try to get the ball into the box.
6. The player who finishes all six holes in the fewest number of strokes wins!

SCOTLAND'S NATIONAL DISH

Haggis is a famous food from Scotland. It is made from the cut-up liver, heart, and lungs of a sheep. These are mixed with oats, salt, onions, and spices. This unusual mixture is then boiled for hours inside a sheep's stomach.

Scottish **cuisine** has many deep-rooted traditions. *Stovies* is a dish made from leftover potatoes, or tatties, and minced beef. Soups are quite popular across Scotland. One variety is Scotch broth. It is typically made with barley, root vegetables, and **mutton**. *Cullen skink* is a soup containing potato, onion, milk, and smoked haddock.

Scotland's many dairy farms create amazing cheeses such as cheddar and Ayrshire Dunlop. A traditional Scottish dessert is *cranachan*. It is made from oatmeal, cream, honey, and raspberries. Popular drinks include tea and an orange soda called Irn-Bru.

CULLEN SKINK

CRANACHAN

SCOTTISH SHORTBREAD

These buttery cookies date back to the 12th century. Make this simple recipe with the help of an adult!

Ingredients:
1/2 cup flour (plus a little extra for your work surface)
3 tablespoons butter, softened
1/2 teaspoon vanilla extract
1/4 cup sugar

Steps:
1. In a medium-sized bowl, use your fingers to combine the flour and butter. The mixture should look like breadcrumbs when you are done.
2. Add in the vanilla and sugar. Stir to combine.
3. Use your hands to squeeze this dough into a ball.
4. Flour the surface you are working on, and roll out the dough until it is about 1/4-inch thick.
5. Use a cookie cutter to cut the dough into shapes. Place these on a cookie sheet lined with parchment paper.
6. Bake the cookies for about 12-15 minutes at 350 degrees Fahrenheit (177 degrees Celsius). They should be a light golden-brown color.
7. Let the cookies cool on a rack. Enjoy!

People in Scotland celebrate a variety of holidays. On November 30, Scots celebrate St. Andrew's Day. This national holiday is the feast of Scotland's **patron saint**. Special events on this day include dances, storytelling, craft markets, and a lot of live music. On Christmas Eve, some Scots burn rowan tree branches. This is meant to show that bad feelings between relatives or friends are put aside.

On New Year's Eve, the city of Edinburgh hosts huge street parties and sing-alongs. There are also incredible fireworks at midnight at Edinburgh Castle. But folks in Scotland celebrate their country and culture throughout the year!

BURNS NIGHT

January 25 is Burns Night in Scotland. On this night, Scots celebrate the birthday of famous Scottish poet Robert Burns. People recite his poems and songs. They also have a terrific feast including haggis and potatoes.

NEW YEAR'S EVE FIREWORKS
IN EDINBURGH

84 CE
The Roman Empire arrives in the area that is now Scotland

1314
Robert the Bruce defeats England at Bannockburn in the First War of Scottish Independence

795
Vikings attack a monastery on the Scottish island of Iona

1040
King Macbeth takes the Scottish throne and rules for more than a decade

1707
The Act of Union is signed, uniting Scotland and England under one Parliament of Great Britain

1999
Scottish Parliament meets for the first time in almost 300 years

1914
Scottish soldiers and steel workers are important to helping the Allies in World War I

2014
Scottish people vote against becoming an independent country

SCOTLAND FACTS

Official Name: Scotland

Flag of Scotland: Scotland's flag is blue and white. On top of the blue background is a white diagonal cross, known as a saltire. The flag is also called St. Andrew's Cross, named after the country's patron saint.

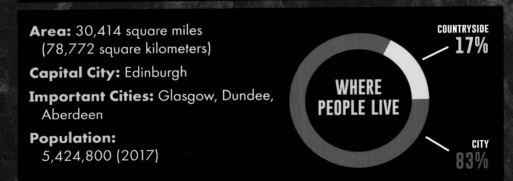

Area: 30,414 square miles
(78,772 square kilometers)

Capital City: Edinburgh

Important Cities: Glasgow, Dundee, Aberdeen

Population:
5,424,800 (2017)

WHERE PEOPLE LIVE

COUNTRYSIDE
17%

CITY
83%

JOBS (FOR THE UK)

SERVICES
83.5%

MANUFACTURING
15.2%

FARMING
1.3%

Main Exports (for the UK):

fuels   food   chemicals

beverages   tobacco   manufactured goods

National Holiday:
St. Andrew's Day (November 30)

Main Languages:
English, Gaelic

Form of Government:
parliamentary constitutional monarchy

Title for Country Leaders:
prime minister (head of government),
queen (head of state)

RELIGION (IN THE UK)

NONE
25.7%

OTHER
10.4%

MUSLIM
4.4%

CHRISTIAN
59.5%

Unit of Money:
Pound sterling (GBP)

GLOSSARY

clans–large groups of families who have common ancestors and are loyal to one another

cuisine–a style of cooking

cultural–relating to the beliefs, arts, and ways of life in a place or society

descent–a person's line of ancestors

loch–the Scottish word for lake

manufacture–to make products, often with machines

moorlands–land made up of ground that is too wet or too poor for farming

mutton–sheep meat

patron saint–a saint who is believed to look after a country or group of people

remote–far removed

rural–related to the countryside

service jobs–jobs that perform tasks for people or businesses

tourism–the business of people traveling to visit other places

traditional–related to customs, ideas, or beliefs passed down from one generation to the next

urban–related to cities and city life

venomous–producing a poisonous substance called venom

TO LEARN MORE

AT THE LIBRARY

Arbuthnott, Gill. *A Secret Diary of The First World War*. UK: Floris Books, 2018.

Greig, Gemma. *United Kingdom*. New York, N.Y.: Cavendish Square Publishing, 2018.

Harrison, Susan. *All About Scotland*. UK: BookLife Publishing, 2015.

ON THE WEB

FACTSURFER

Factsurfer.com gives you a safe, fun way to find more information.

1. Go to www.factsurfer.com.

2. Enter "Scotland" into the search box and click 🔍.

3. Select your book cover to see a list of related web sites.

INDEX

The images in this book are reproduced through the courtesy of: Dan Breckwoldt, cover; Lee Gillion, pp. 4-5; Tetiana Dickens, p. 5 (top); Sprioview Inc, p. 5 (top middle); Spunmador, p. 5 (bottom middle); George KUZ, p. 5 (bottom); AridOcean, pp. 6-7, 8; Kasefoto, p. 8; eye35/ Alamy, p. 9; evenfh, p. 9 (right); Eric Isselee, p. 10 (left); Marek Kania, p. 10 (top); Ian McDonald, p. 10 (top middle); Mark Medcalf, p. 10 (middle bottom); Abi Warner, p. 10 (bottom); Andrew M. Allport, pp. 10-11; Richard Wood/ Alamy, p. 12; Featureflash Photo Agency, p. 13 (top); David Boutin, p. 13; Brendan Howard, p. 14; Lukassek, p. 15; David Kilpatrick/ Alamy, p. 16; Imladris, p. 17; Colin McPherson/ Getty, pp. 18, 27 (top); JasperImage, pp. 19 (top), 21; Chris James/ Alamy, p. 19; Neil G Paterson/ Alamy, p. 20; Mai Groves, p. 20; National Geographic Image Collection/ Alamy, p. 22; Joerg Beuge, p. 23 (top, middle); Martin Rettenberger, p. 23 (bottom); Gary Doak/ Alamy, p. 24; jmimages, p. 25; Chronicle/ Alamy, p. 26 (top); Brobra694/ Wiki Commons, p. 26 (bottom); Jeff Gilbert/ Alamy, p. 27 (bottom); PhotoEdit/ Alamy, p. 29; Fat Jackey, p. 29 (right).